Jenn

A Whole Bunch of
Feelings
What do they mean?

BARRON'S

Cont

I Feel Calm

Feeling calm is when your body is still and your thoughts are quiet, **like floating on a cloud.**
Sometimes when my heart is beating fast and my body is tense, I have to take three deep breaths, in through my nose and out through my mouth. When my breathing slows down, my voice is soft, and my arms and legs are loose; I am calm.

Sitting by a warm, cozy fire, staring up at a starry night makes me feel calm. Ahhh.

My Dog Feels Frisky!

Did you know that when I get home from school, my dog gets so frisky? **He's so happy,** he even looks like he's smiling. Sometimes when my dog feels really frisky, he'll find his favorite toy, pick it up in his mouth, shake it, and then fling it high up in the air.

Feeling goofy and silly and full of energy is a happy and fun feeling.

I Feel Cozy!

I feel so cozy when I am all snuggled into my bed with my favorite doll Keisha. Getting tucked into my bed with my fluffy blanket makes me feel warm and comfy, especially when it is cold outside. **There is nothing more special than being cuddled up close to someone you love,** making you feel safe and all fuzzy inside. Now that is cozy!

What makes you feel cozy?

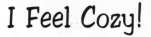

9

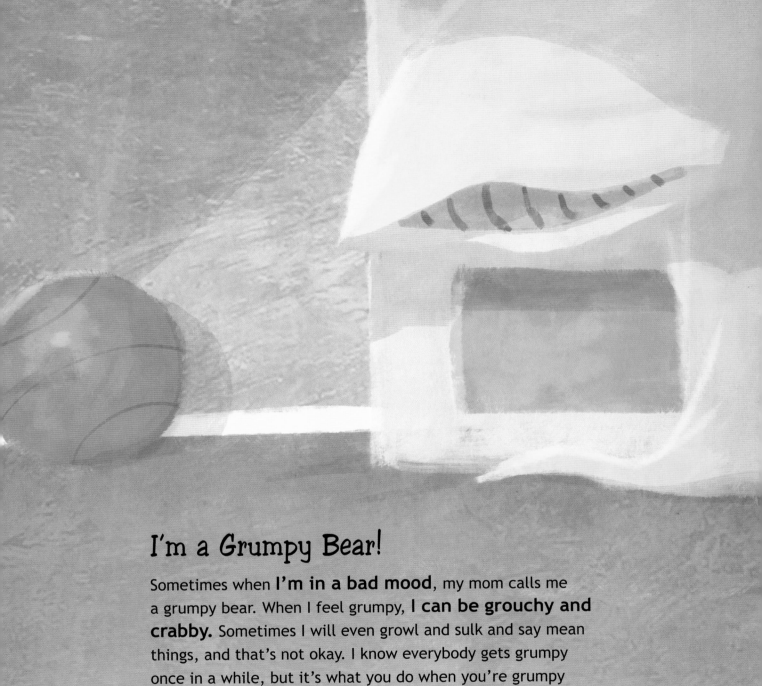

I'm a Grumpy Bear!

Sometimes when **I'm in a bad mood**, my mom calls me a grumpy bear. When I feel grumpy, **I can be grouchy and crabby.** Sometimes I will even growl and sulk and say mean things, and that's not okay. I know everybody gets grumpy once in a while, but it's what you do when you're grumpy that matters. Going to a quiet place by myself or going for a walk helps get rid of the grumpy bear inside me.

What do you do when you feel cranky and grumpy?

Mr. Sloth Feels Lazy

Did you know that Mr. Sloth always feels lazy? He's slow and sluggish and **just wants to lay around and do nothing at all.** Sometimes when Mr. Sloth feels lazy, and he has to get up and get moving, it takes all his energy to get things done. It's okay to be quiet and lazy once in a while, but when it's time to get going, it's time to get going!

Do you ever feel lazy?

Mike Feels Anticipation!

Mike gets so excited when he turns Jack's crank
and the music starts to play. Mike feels anticipation
when he's waiting for Jack to jump out of his box.
The surprised look on Mike's face when Jack springs
out of the box, high into the air, makes everybody laugh.
This feeling of anticipation is the same feeling you get
the night before your birthday party, when you
can't wait to open your gifts.

Anticipation; how fun!

I'm So Disappointed!

Have you ever really, really wanted to do something and for some reason you couldn't do it? The feeling you get when this happens is called disappointment. I was so disappointed when my best friend and I planned to go to the park but **we couldn't go because a big thunderstorm came.** Instead of staying sad and upset though, we found some other fun activity to do.

What do you do when you feel disappointed?

I'm So Proud!

With shiny new red paint, my race car waits for the flag to drop to start the race. They're off! My race car zooms around the track, **trying so hard to win.** Then after 4 laps, my race car wins! Have you ever worked so hard to do something and then you did it? That's what it feels like to be proud. With a sparkly gold medal, I feel proud.

Hooray, I did it!

19

I Feel Safe

My mom and dad make me feel safe, **because they are always there for me.** They look after me when I am sick; they let me crawl into their bed when I have a bad dream and I'm scared; and, when we go out in the car, they make sure I am buckled into my car seat, safe and sound.

What makes you feel safe?

Guilty!

Have you ever done something that you knew you weren't supposed to do, like telling a lie or taking a cookie from the cookie jar? Then after it happens you feel bad about it. Whenever my puppy gets caught doing something that he knows is wrong, like chewing on my shoe, he feels guilty. He looks at me with big eyes, droopy ears, and he puts his tail between his legs. Feeling guilty is not a good feeling and that's why if you ever feel guilty about something you have done, try to make it right.

And then try not to do it again!

Mother Nature Is Feeling Joyful Today!

When the sun is shining, there's a warm breeze and the birds are singing, that's when you know Mother Nature is feeling joyful. And when Mother Nature is joyful, she makes everybody feel happy and free like a white fluffy cloud floating across the sky. Joyful is a good feeling, so **find one thing every day that makes you feel joy and happiness.**

Smile!

Jealousy Is an Ugly Thing!

When somebody has something that you really want and you don't have, that's what it feels like to be jealous. I really wanted to get an A on my spelling test, but instead I got a B and my friend got the A. This made me feel mad and jealous. Did you know that sometimes when a person feels mad and jealous, they can do and say mean things? Jealousy is a bad feeling and **it's never okay to do mean things to another person.**

Be happy with what you have and try not to worry about what you do not have!

Nervous Nelly,
the Skittish Fawn

Did you know that fawns can feel skittish? Have you ever seen a baby deer, looking a little scared, running from tree to tree trying to hide, especially when there are people around? Whenever Nelly is in the meadow and she hears a noise, she feels jumpy and a little nervous. **That's when she runs as fast as she can to her mother's side.** Being close to her mother helps make Nelly feel better.

What makes you feel skittish?

Tense Like a Rubber Band

Have you ever tried to stretch a rubber band and no matter how hard you tried, the band was so tight it could not be stretched? Sometimes when I feel tense and stressed, **my muscles get all tight and stiff.** This usually happens when I go to the dentist and I am feeling a little scared and nervous.

Taking a deep breath helps my muscles relax.

Sometimes I Feel Worried

Sometimes I am bothered and can't stop thinking about something, like how I'm going to do on my next math test, or what's going to happen when my brother finds out that I broke his bike.

That's when I know I have to do something to make things better. Feeling worried and nervous and scared is not a good feeling, but I know if I study harder and tell the truth, most of my worries will go away.

What is something you worry about?

It's So Frustrating

Have you ever tried to do something and, no matter how hard you tried, you just couldn't do it? Just like **a spinning top that tries to keep spinning** but after a while it tips over. It can be so frustrating and make you so mad that you just want to give up, but don't forget that if you keep trying, you just might get it.

Can you think of a time when you felt frustrated and wanted to give up trying?

The Ducklings Feel Loved

Mama duck takes good care of her ducklings. She takes them for slow paddles down the river and **always makes sure they have everything they need to feel safe, happy, and content.** Mama duck tells her ducklings every day how much she loves them. It's a good feeling to know that somebody cares about you.

Who makes you feel loved?

The Ball of Dread

Dread is a lot of bad feelings. **It is being really scared, really worried, and really nervous,** all rolled into one big ball. Sometimes I feel dread when it's time to go to bed during a lightning storm. Whenever I see the lightning bolts and feel the rumbling of the sky, my heart starts to beat really fast and I get all sweaty. Sometimes the only way I can stop shaking is to hide underneath my blankets.

What makes you feel dread?

Ecstatic, How Exciting!

I had a dream that I was a rock star and hundreds of people came to hear me sing. **When I came out onto the stage, the crowd went wild!** The crowd was so excited and happy; they cheered and clapped, and jumped up and down. Feeling ecstatic is a powerful feeling!

Have you ever felt so much excitement that you felt like you were going to burst?

41

I Don't Like to Feel Ashamed

It feels really terrible when you know that you did something wrong, like blaming your friend for something she didn't do and getting her in trouble for it. It doesn't feel good **when all you want to do is hide your head** because you feel so sad and sorry for what you did.

Saying that you are sorry and will never do it again can sometimes make things right again!

42

I Feel Embarrassed

I will never forget how embarrassed I felt when I went down the waterslide so fast that my bathing suit ripped! When I got out of the pool, **my face turned all red and hot.** I felt awkward trying to hide the hole in my suit and I just wanted to hide. The funny part is that nobody else noticed the hole but me.

Have you ever felt embarrassed before?

44

The Silly Clown!

Clowns always feel silly! They do funny things to make us laugh, like tripping over their big shoes, wearing colorful clothes, and making funny faces. When I feel silly, **it feels like there's a bubble in my tummy** and, when the bubble suddenly bursts, I like to giggle and dance around all wild and crazy.

It's okay to be silly once in a while.

I Feel Impatient

When I'm in a hurry and all the other children
in the line are moving too slowly, it makes me mad and
irritated. Whenever this happens, I stamp my feet and feel
like yelling out for everybody to get moving!

Sometimes it is really hard to wait!
What makes you feel impatient?

Mr. Shy Guy

Have you ever gone to a new place where there are lots of people you don't know and all of a sudden you feel like you want to hide under a table? Whenever I meet somebody new and they say "Hi" to me, I get really quiet. I look away and **sometimes I even try to hide my face.** When this happens to me, my mom says I am being Mr. Shy Guy.

What makes you feel shy?

Confused!

Have you ever felt like you didn't know **what to do or which way to go,** and the more you tried to figure things out the worse it got? Sometimes I get so confused when I'm driving my train and there are so many tracks to choose from. I get all mixed up and never know which track to pick because each track goes in a different direction. When I'm really stuck and don't know what to do, I ask my brother for help.

Everybody needs a little help sometimes to make things clearer.

53

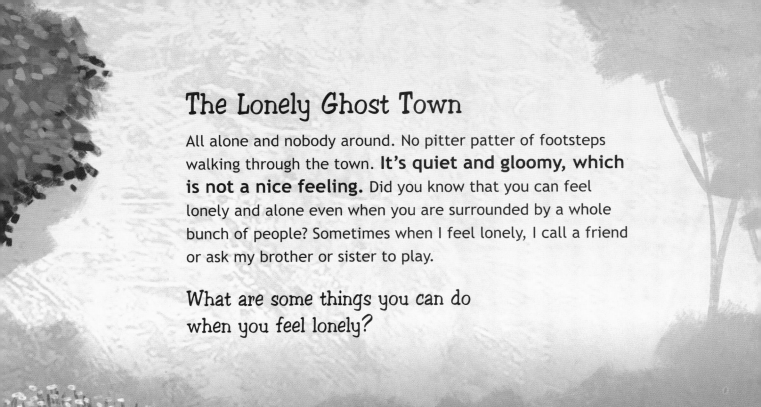

The Lonely Ghost Town

All alone and nobody around. No pitter patter of footsteps walking through the town. **It's quiet and gloomy, which is not a nice feeling.** Did you know that you can feel lonely and alone even when you are surrounded by a whole bunch of people? Sometimes when I feel lonely, I call a friend or ask my brother or sister to play.

What are some things you can do when you feel lonely?

Swimming Scared

Have you ever tried to learn something new that really scared you? Learning to swim really scared me. At first, whenever I went close to water, like a pool or a beach, my eyes would get really big. **I would cry and just want to run away.** But do you know that it's normal to be scared of learning new things? And guess what? I took my time and practiced with my swim teacher and now I love swimming. I overcame my fear!

What is something that scares you?

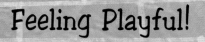

Feeling Playful!

Have you ever seen a kitten sit still? Me neither! Kittens are always busy, running around, chasing their tails, pouncing, and wrestling each other. Sometimes when kittens are feeling so lively and full of spunk, they can get into mischief, like getting tangled up in a ball of yarn.

Kittens just want to have fun! Feeling playful is such a good feeling!

I Feel Blah!

Sometimes on a cold, rainy day when there is nothing to do, I feel blah. **I don't have any energy, and I'm tired and slow.** I don't feel happy or sad, I just feel blah! The best way to get rid of the feeling of nothingness is to get up and get moving. Maybe call a friend or pick up a good book.

No matter what, just start doing something.

The Fuming Mad Tea Kettle

Have you ever seen a boiling tea kettle? It's smoldering hot with steam billowing everywhere and it looks like the lid is going to pop off! Feeling fuming mad is a problem feeling and it is a bigger feeling than just mad. **It feels like you might explode.** Unlike a tea kettle, we can't just stop simmering, but we do need to stop. Try taking a few deep breaths to relax your body.

We can't solve any problems when we are so full of anger.

63

Mischievous Ricky

Ricky the Raccoon loves to explore but **sometimes his curiosity gets him into trouble,** especially when he wants to find out what yummy treasures he can find in a garbage can. When Ricky misbehaves by knocking over a garbage can, he feels playful and sneaky, and even a little naughty all at the same time.

Do you ever feel mischievous?

I'm So Thankful!

Whenever I bring my teddy bear with me to school, I feel so happy and relieved to have him with me because then I'm not alone. I am grateful to see him snuggled into my backpack while we ride the bus together to school. Have you ever felt so happy to have something, that you couldn't stop saying "Thank you"? **Feeling thankful is a warm feeling.**

It's important to show our gratitude with a hug, a "thank you," or even a special note.

I Feel Brave!

Have you ever had to do something that really scared you, but you knew that it was the right thing to do? That's what it feels like to be brave. I remember when I lost my sister's favorite barrette, it took a lot of courage to tell the truth about what happened. My sister was sad about her barrette, but she was happy that I told her the truth.

Have you ever had to do something that was really hard to do, but you knew it had to be done?

69

I Feel Heartbroken

Have you ever felt so, so sad that it actually felt like your heart was breaking? It hurts! I remember when my dog Rusty got sick and didn't get better. I was so upset and felt like I would never smile again. When my friends tried to make me feel better, no matter what they did or said, nothing helped. **I was completely crushed and couldn't stop crying.** As time passed I started to feel better.

I will never forget Rusty and how heartbroken I was when he was gone.

The Bully at School
Makes Me Feel Intimidated

Every day at lunch, Billy the Bully comes over to my table and gives me **a mean and scary look** because he wants me to give him the cookies in my lunch box. I don't want to give him my cookies, but Billy hassles and scares me, especially when he stares at me and speaks in a mean voice. Feeling intimidated is not a good feeling.

It's a feeling that tells you that you need to ask an adult for help.

I'm Bored!

Everybody has felt bored once in a while. You know when you feel like there is nothing to do and **nothing seems interesting or fun.** Then all you can say is "I'm bored." That's when we need to find something to do. Did you know that feeling bored is a great opportunity to try something new.

The funny part is that once you start doing something, you actually forget that you were bored.

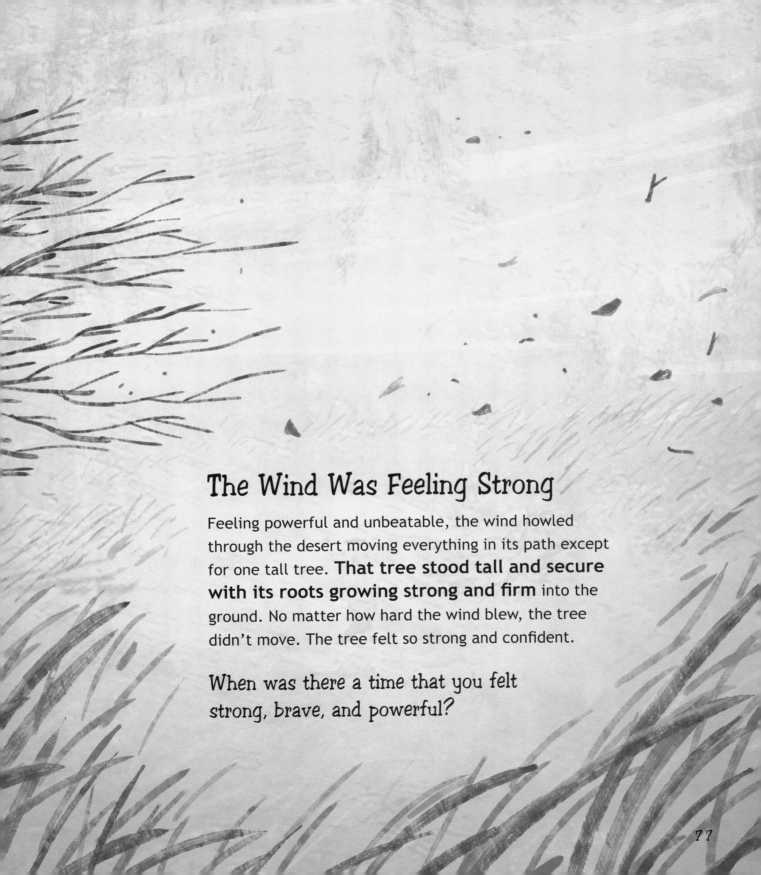

The Wind Was Feeling Strong

Feeling powerful and unbeatable, the wind howled through the desert moving everything in its path except for one tall tree. **That tree stood tall and secure with its roots growing strong and firm** into the ground. No matter how hard the wind blew, the tree didn't move. The tree felt so strong and confident.

When was there a time that you felt strong, brave, and powerful?

Content Like My Sleeping Baby Brother

Have you ever seen a sleeping baby? Whenever my brother is sleeping, **he looks so peaceful and happy.** Right before he goes to bed, he is bathed in warm water and given a bottle. Then he cuddles up all safe and sound in his crib. Warm clothes and a full belly make my brother feel content. He has everything he needs, plus a lot of love.

What makes you feel content?

The Spider Felt So Diligent

After the spider worked so hard and finished spinning his web, he felt so accomplished that he began working on another web. He always pays close attention to the details. He spins his thread so carefully, making sure the web is perfect. Feeling diligent is a good feeling. It's the feeling you get **when you put extra time and care into doing something in the best way possible.**

When have you felt diligent?

Sometimes My Turtle Feels Withdrawn

I know when my pet turtle Chipper wants to be alone and away from people, because he goes into his shell. Feeling quiet, and reserved, he stays in his shell until he feels like playing again. At first I couldn't understand why Chipper didn't want to be my friend, but now I know that **it is okay for him to want some alone time.**

When he is ready, he will come out of his shell.

Awkward

Have you ever tried to do something new and you felt a little foolish? I remember when I first learned how to skate, everything felt new. My ice skates felt funny on my feet. Not only was it hard to walk, but when I started to ice skate, I felt like I was going to trip over my own two feet. **After a lot of practice, things got easier** and I got a lot better and I feel good ice skating now!

Have you ever felt awkward doing something new?

I Feel So Rotten!

Have you ever eaten too much candy and afterward you felt yucky? This happened to me once and not only did I feel terrible because I ate all the candy, but I also felt bad that I didn't listen to my mom. It is a bad feeling **to feel so horrible about doing something you know you should not have done.** Next time it might be a better idea to listen to my mom.

Have you ever felt rotten about doing something that maybe you shouldn't have done?

I'm Sorry!

Have you ever done something that you didn't mean to do? One time I accidently tripped over my friend's Lego tower and broke it. **I felt sad that I ruined my friend's tower and that I hurt his feelings.** I told him that I was sorry and that I would be more careful next time.

When we worked together to rebuild the tower, it helped make everything right again.

My Baby Sister Is Curious!

Have you ever seen a baby looking curious?
My baby sister loves to learn about the world around her.
With big eyes, she crawls around and explores. Whenever my sister is really curious, she uses her hands to touch things, uses her nose to smell things, and sometimes even puts things in her mouth. We have to watch out for that! Being curious helps us learn and everybody knows that **learning about new things is always fun!**

Are you curious?

Feelings, Feelings, Feelings!!!

Did you know that everybody has feelings? There are good feelings like happy, surprised, and excited, and then there are problem feelings like sad, mad, and frustrated. **When you have happy feelings enjoy them!** And when you have a problem feeling, it means you have to solve the problem so that you will feel better.

But no matter how you are feeling,
that feeling belongs to you.

How Do You Feel Today?

A Whole Bunch of
Feelings
What do they mean?

First edition for the United States and Canada published in 2018 by
Barron's Educational Series, Inc.
Original title of the book in English:
A Whole Bunch of Feelings: What Do They Mean?
© Copyright GEMSER PUBLICATIONS S.L., 2018
c/Castell, 38; Teià(08329) Barcelona, Spain (World Rights)
Tel: 93 540 13 53
E-mail: *info@mercedesros.com*
Website: *www.mercedesros.com*
Author: Jennifer Moore-Mallinos
Illustrator: Gustavo Mazali

ISBN: 978-1-4380-1147-9
Library of Congress Control No.: 2017945591

All inquiries should be addressed to:
Barron's Educational Series, Inc.
250 Wireless Boulevard
Hauppauge, NY 11788
www.barronseduc.com

Manufactured by: L. Rex Printing Company Limited, Dongguan, China
Date of Manufacture: December 2017

Printed in China
9 8 7 6 5 4 3 2 1